STARK NAKED BLUES

By the Same Author

From Raven Arts Press

The Restless Factor
The Way the Money Goes
Small Sky, Big Change

Stark Naked Blues

Aidan Murphy

AIDAN
MURPHY

**N E W
ISLAND
BOOKS**

DUBLIN

Stark Naked Blues
is first published in 1997
in Ireland by
New Island Books,
2 Brookside,
Dundrum Road,
Dublin 14,
Ireland.

Copyright © Aidan Murphy, 1997

ISBN 1 874597 67 7

Grant-aided by the
Arts Council

New Island Books receives financial assistance from **The
Arts Council (An Chomhairle Ealaíon)**, Dublin, Ireland.
The author also wishes to thank the Arts Council of Ireland
for a Bursary in 1991 and Art Flights in 1991 and 1994 which
assisted the writing of some of these poems.

Cover design by Jon Berkeley
Typeset by Graphic Resources
Printed in Ireland by Colour Books, Ltd.

CONTENTS

*For Colette Daly, Humphrey Sorensen,
Kevin Healy and Philip Casey.
Thanks for the fresh horses.*

SANCTUARY

When I walk in the door
they smell my dismay.
It's cool, son, they say,
we have been here forever.
And it's true. Whatever your crime
there is someone here who did it.

These are living mirrors,
these are my dour accomplices,
these are my brothers who laugh
for the sake of the sound of it.
Step inside, Greta,
don't be bashful,
there are diversions here
amongst the wreckage.

Soon, the joint fills,
and as the woods of pain encroach
we keep our needles clean, pointed,
ever-ready with jolts of light
and slick surreal yarns. In here
the main event is over,
the palaver is done, so

don't cry hon, the torches of dawn
were never as bright
as the sun in your heart,
and the names we might have made
less solid than this swirling ice.
Known by all and none
let this be our raft of the moment,
bobbing on these queasy waters
not-so-young lovers anymore.

THE HABITS OF GUILT

It summons up schooldays in the abattoir.
It scalds your lungs with unwanted smoke
as it thumbs up your eyelids in the small hours
chaining you to the bleakest sounds
of wind, rain and broken homes.

Smooching beside you
with its tongue in your ear, it somehow whispers,
if you weren't so dumb in the first place
I wouldn't be here; then, gargling
a barrel of nails it staggers from bed
with sleep-yellow eyes and insecticide veins.

On the verge of your most brilliant punchlines
it cackles, bursting into brazen mockery,
ripping the airvalves of your resources,
completing the ruin of your confidence.

But it can be so nice to come home to...

with its pipe and slippers and cosseting cushions
dispensing permission to weep indulgently
as its barbs inflict delicious pain.

NIGHT PAINTING

Low in the river
the swans are sleeping
with their necks tucked
under oil-spattered wings

A drunken car swings
uphill through the fog
and out the rolled-down glass
a waitress pukes

In doorways the young
are kissing   holding hands
bathing in imaginary seams
and unzipped jeans

Mascara'd witch
the city blinks
bubbling and brewing
stews of trouble

In the back of the Volks
I touch your bruised thigh
as you raise the open bottle
to my parted lips

A WALTZ IN WHISKEY TIME

I couldn't believe my eyes
she was a midget
a hunchback too
tossing back neat vodkas
like she couldn't give a damn
about the telescopes
spying from the vol-au-vent

So I tranced across the floor
and chanced my arm
she said she knew me
and when I asked her who I was
she spat a jet of Huzzar
on the Persian cat
said you're a scream you are

I was trying to figure
the way back home
when big mama in the kitchen
started shouting
about the bitch's drinking habits
and all-night fornications
and when the bride's father
a temperamental Irish-Italian
and a breeder of champion ferrets
smashed a fist through the window
just missing the midget's jaw
I rushed out the backdoor
and turned into a crow
with shiny feathers

You explode. I forgive.
I protest. You forget.
Neck-in-neck we ride, misunderstood.
A lull in communication lifts the window,
carries you away over the city and its tributaries,
over the black sea without a signal light,
and a fierce silence troubles me.
I try to take stock of the place and year
but there are too many shadows here
so I grab the cash, strap on the Walkman
and stroll down the hill to quench my fear.
To comfort you later I bring
what I imagine you want,
but it is never yours.
Take it back, you say, take it away.

Is there somewhere we can meet we've never met
    before
and not United Avenue, not Sucker's Square?

LATE LOVE

I understand her better now she's dead.
It's easier plucking strands of her out of the air
when she can't oppose the stuff I choose.
Composing her remains I'll soon have a finished
   piece.

When she was alive she couldn't help
acting out of character,
doing the odd thing for the sake of it.
When she was alive she moved too much.
One time a single eye-blink set me back by years,
but death has ended all those restless urges.

Revisiting old ground I sift
the solid from the shade, without rebuke.
She's finally coming together.
If only she would breathe this time
I think I could love her forever.

THE YEAR OF THE WIND

In the year of the wind
I was miles from the heartland,
goon-eyed under a crooked vine
with nothing to write home about.

The world was out of season,
a long street of gales and swooping leaves
in an age of urchins bawling
over dirty redbrick balconies,
and blue lights cutting corners,
arresting intrigue.

There was vagueness everywhere.
Multi-channel days
and nights of stunned silence,
profundity doused in a lather
of crude jokes and neat Scotch.

And death was a cheeky pup
pacing your roof,
stuffing its maw
with chunks of misfortune,
getting heavier above your head,
getting heavier above us all.

TELEGRAM

worn to a thread from sacrifice
he went north
to the mountains to rest
and there
in one agonising motion
of planetary jive
he died

he never said
or did
anything of consequence
nothing
nothing but a light blowing out
as the wind rolled in from the bay
and the stars dripped down
extraordinary calm

WAITING ROOM

The yellow-vested Yankee
and his thousand dollar wife
are reading *Life*. Junior
rabbit-bites a chocolate square.
Cigarette smoke screens the window
from trainless tracks, strips
of neon stitching stone and steel.
On the wall-bench
finished crosswords curl up
under the hot air fan,
among suitcases, cameras, plastic bags.
An old man shuffles in
carrying a wizened brown case
treble-tied with scraps of string,
sits and pulls out black beads,
prays decade after decade,
lip-sounds like a wounded bee.

THE FIDDLER

after a painting by Diarmuid Ó Ceallacháin

He is charming the light
from river and sky,
levitating above the grey bridge
and its resident beggars,
leaving the city to its plight
of errant flesh and dour smudges.

It's just another afternoon
of business, work and worry,
blurring the wild tune he plays
that coaxes the sun to flow in
from his feet to his clear high brow,
where it detonates and becomes
a flame-yellow ladder
for the earthbound.

Mother, why is the bird singing?
Father, who is the bird singing to?
Mother, Father, what is the bird saying?

The bird is quiet now.
Only the child's voice fills the wood.
Bewildered silence stitches mother's lips.
Ships of knowledge sink in father's heart.

The nations of the earth
are gathered in a pentagon of leaves.
Their questions pass from mouth to mouth
and dry twigs snap.

Why? Who? What?
Unanimous shaking of heads.
Unanimous ignorance winds thick vines
round the bird's stopped heart.

SCIENCE

Conditions are ideal.
The room is soundproof,
the temperature is
cool enough for clear thought.

No expense has been spared.
From the smallest screw
to the crudest fixture
the equipment gleams
in virgin straw.

Still, the vital step eludes him,
stops him like a bombed bridge.
The broken neck of logic
swings above a deep ravine.

Outside the glass laboratory
the ocean hammers at the shore,
each wave riding off
with slivers of hard fact.

THE FUTURE PERFECT

Whatever falls will land feet up
in pre-allocated space.
Just imagine, objects, persons too
unable to elude comprehension,
unable to dissent. All things
unbreakable and rigidly fixed.

We'll sit, greyhaired and grinning,
watching videos of bygone days,
moderately humoured by the chaos,
the mobs of contentious mouths,
the furrows of the intelligentsia;
all that fuss of yesteryear.

Over dinner someone will allude
to the latest slapstick,
The Pursuit of Meaning, and the guests
will crack up. It couldn't be jollier,
eternal daylight. Night will have been
long syphoned off into glass casks,
for curiosity value.

THE END OF THE TWENTIETH CENTURY

Mr Smith is not going to Washington

Mr Smith
is going brown

Disintegrating
into highly-combustible powder

Bleeding nitrates

Murdered by moisture

Mr Smith is not going to Washington

Mr Smith
is dying

In a vault
in Dayton Ohio

People invariably get me wrong.
They mistake me
for a deep blue pool
on a hot August day
and dive right in.
They like to make a big splash.
Sure I get tired
but I'll smoke their brands
and nod in all the right places
and make appropriate fishy O's
and tut-tut at the debts and doom.
They dig all that
the clichés stinking of truth.
The little man goes home
to the little woman
with a beer belly
and a lighter conscience
as if his sins had just been eaten
by the craggy stranger
whose face he can't quite remember
as he slides into sleep
absolved by its cool surface.
I've an adjustable waveband in my head.
I've yet to find a misery
I can't tune into
chew it up and spit it back
in a neat envelope.
I don't do favours no more
at least not in the active sense
like the old days.
No more guns blazing
downtown in the noon heat
no more roadblocks

and double-crossing dames.
Now I'm more like that wailing wall
smeared with pressures and problems
but still standing.
Sure I get weary
but I don't like to talk about that.

the girl in the photo
is smiling like
the young Katherine Hepburn
picnicking
on a lush cliff somewhere
beside a tall dark man
the clouds flying
on a string from a child's finger
there's wheaten bread
and cheese
milked tea and warm cider
unlike the downpour later
after they touched and kissed

THE WOMAN IN THE FISHING TACKLE SHOP

The woman in the fishing tackle shop
is beat. She drank a tank again
last night. Hammocks of despair
beneath her eyes, above a fishnet
brown and green. Anytime before six
she'll sell you hooks, lines and sinkers,
but when she pulls those blinds
schools of headless fish follow her
upstairs to the rarely dusted room
where she drowns in her aquarium of stars.

THE INCONSOLABLE

Her face buried in her hands
The tears flowing through her slender fingers
Red ants floundering in the chocolate pudding
The sun beating mallets on the parched city
Geysers of sweat under her arms
The baby bawling with a lobster rash
The baby wheezing with a cold in his chest
The milk slapped sour in the sink
Her face buried in her hands
The tears soaking into her knuckles
She is crying for the impossible
She has grown to the size of the earth
She is stretched across all possible space
Now there is no more room
Now she cannot scratch the itch that lingers
Now she cannot catch the ripest plum
Her sadness is a gold nugget gleaming
At the feet of a blind pauper

SURVIVAL

Space stretches
between the hours,
the seconds beat
a weakened heart.

His face seeks comfort
in his hands, then
through his fingers he sees
a street of others like himself,
how unexceptional he is.

Soon after this
he learns to move
without haste or hesitation,
but casual, brilliant,
like a rat.

SPEED

Dreams are ending everywhere.
Sleepers are anxious
to hurry out
into the loud ambitious light,
to forget sinister implications,
to leave me here alone
among my crumpled failures,
not worth a spit.

I could go on strike,
demand longer nights,
extended solitude.
But my name carries no weight,
and even as I plead
the bastards are filling
the syringes with tomorrow.

DIVORCE

They should have been gone
when the sun rose
on the makeshift beds
but there was an hour's delay
before the murder of the future,
an hour of rummaging through
less certain possessions.
How absurd,
she thought, the toothpaste
never stung like this before.
A neutral person came
to referee the furniture,
and the score at full time
was a foul-tongue-all.

MAN TALK

My first wife never made me jelly.
Exceptional in warmth and wit,
miraculous with bread and fish,
I hadn't the heart to tell her
my singular obsessive wish,

a mould of wobbling scarlet or
transparent green. One ice-cold
spoonful of that prismatic flesh
would have kept me grateful, faithful.

VISITING RIGHTS

The fathers have eaten sour grapes
and the children's teeth are set on edge.

Somehow these are his finest hours,
when the kids swing high on the iron galleon
and the sunlight on their handsome limbs
adds mawkish splendour.

The youngest waves, smiles back
at the old-man bench where he sits
guzzling beer, swallowing gobs of self-pity,
trying hard to quit

making sense of the uncivil wars,
the various gestures, words and moods
that have ordained this dazzling judgement day.

Obstacles on a bright May morning,
how to dislodge
a sliver of putrid ham
from a back tooth
with an anaesthetised tongue,
contend with nightmares of infidelity
and a brand new penniless day.
Taking no chances
I climb from the bed
with a rope around my waist.
It's a long way down,
an odyssey between feet and shoes.
Reluctantly I dress, swallow my pint
of VP and grope downstairs to Hollywood.
She's forever at the sink chopping vegetables,
her face caked in Max Factor,
her streaked hair in a net.
There's a plea on the box for victims
of cerebral palsy. Ungrateful wretch, says Holly,
you don't know how lucky you are,
her purple eyes weeping onion juice.
My breath stinks. On the tv screen
another heartless hostess with an airline smile
says Listerene is best. But I'd smother
my mother for an ice-cold beer.

75 MUSCLES

After a drink
or five or six
no one's silent
at the same time

Hammers come down
on the troughs of life
tongues picking threads
from the night's sleeve
fluff on the needle
jumpy repeats and slurs

75 muscles
it says on the beer-mat
to make a solitary word

In which case
it's like a sweatshop here
Mr and Mrs Alphabet
pumping iron

75 muscles
Dear God what does it mean
I'd keep my mouth shut
but I can't breathe

HEYDAY

The fireplace pillars are cracked and broken
and the mirror needs rubbing to make a clear picture.
She lifts another glass and talks about the heyday.

I remember, she says. I remember
you couldn't get inside the doors in those days.
There's woeful creatures living here now,
the house down the road suspiciously gutted,
what class of a world has been loosed on us?
what kind of people would do those things?
a couple of unsolved killings and ear-choppings
not to mention the bag-grabs and the cars burning
strange candles in the night outside our bedrooms.

The Six One News
shuts up the room,
gags the halcyon years,
pours redundancies and blood
on the stained shagpile,
hooks every eye
in its magnetic field.

She peels a photo from her gallery of the dead
and stares at the discolouration, the over-exposure,
and behind the webs she finds a young man and
  woman
whose laughing faces flame with heated plans.
Such was me, she thinks aloud, but no one's listening
as she shivers from the cold in her bones
and the cold cloud gathering above her head
in the opaque mirrors of her stormed palace.

ELEGY FOR THE OTHER

Somewhere I have lost you,
king of the slow smile.
In childhood gardens
burning with energy, arrogance,
you were my sidekick.
We licked the apples
and the grasses clean,
restoring sight
to a suburb of blind windows.
You'd never take no for an answer,
question the swallow's flight
and the moon's constancy, rant
against the hand-me-down phrases
that threatened to curtail your appetite,
from which nothing was safe,
to which everything was sacred.
Where did you go?
Where did you go when you snuck
from this cube of duplicity and blight
where minds play constant tennis of returned serves
and light is ground in tubes of tungsten?

Away from the scourge of daylight we sit,
transfixed by man-made darkness and uncomplex
  calm,
in hieroglyphic poses. I am the Jackal, confounded,
you are the Ibis scarred by your greed for beauty,
and we watch, with other beasts, our lives departing
into the tunnel of the original mystery tour.
We drink to their final journeys,
to the tattered passports of our souls,
and pray that mercy has a sense of humour.

Immured in space, voids of banter
orbit between our elbows,
feeding on photons of strain and silence,
and all that was said before is said again,
the reason and the rubbish, the smashing of promises,
in the cultivated language of destruction,
while we suck each other's bruises
and find each other always on a fallow footing.

Once was the heady green of possibility
sprouting earthly peace.
Once was an open book
loaded with restful heat.
But the seeds of deceit had been planted,
the white pages waiting to burn.

Now, as we relate
our singular falls,
browbeaten Jackal to ageing Ibis,
our eyes become a single eye,
a telescope of pain and longing
scouring earth sea and sky for our cunning.

Now, the screen hollers death in vivid Kodachrome,
and the corpulent general informs the room
that he, also, doesn't give a rat's butt.
This is how it is, how it must be;
the kerb beyond the door is cracking, oozing gas.
We drink again and breathe it in,
and breathe it in,
and breathe it in...

THE STONE MAN

Here in Calcutta
dosed on excrement
I see too much.
Disease drags through me
searching for a shrine.
Three-legged dogs
whose backs I have broken
refuse to lie down
but howl in my head
and keep me sleepless.
I cross the lobby
into a hell
of beseeching hands
and human shit
and I give them this day
their peace prize
in the shape of a stone.
To date I have silenced
eleven wretched souls
demoralised empty-bellied beings
whose prayers went unanswered
who are not missed.
I sip iced beer on my hotel balcony
and still I see too much.
I have done so little.
There is so much left to do.

DEATH OF A TYRANT

First you kicked the soil,
the dog, and then your son
hard on the shin.

I saw it all from my pillbox
with that tick between your braces
in my sights.

   I saw you
building fences and sealing doors,
locking pennies in brown boxes,
scowling at your daughter
with a thick belt in your fist.

You don't know me yet,
I'm not spittle to scorn.
I'm death,
  you bitter bald fool,
the man in the bright pyjamas
come now without a gun
to finally arrest your heart
and run off with your puny hoard.

CLASSICAL MUSIC

She turned her grief to the green star,
the only one raining on London.
She picked up the bottle
and smashed the guitar.
The neighbours, perturbed by the music,
screamed Turn It Down, Turn It Down.
She took off her crown.
She filled up the bath and then
sleepily drowned.
That's better, they sighed. Classical Music.

THERE GOES THE NEIGHBOURHOOD

I was sawing my darling
in half when I saw him,
the pious quack from number nine,
peering through the kitchen glass,
leering and licking his cracked lips
with a bright red relish,
his eyes like a couple of lenses
daubed in blood.
I knew he wouldn't see
the radiance spurting from her midriff
in all its fragrant glory.
I knew by those eyes that he'd panic
and dial emergency.

MAN AT A WINDOW

On the canvas of oblong glass
three leaves on the tree.
The sky stops dead above the roof.
The street runs north to south
where I will never go.
This is the terminus,
my exquisite cell.

I paint the walls with sour cream.
I tape the Chinese torture of the tap.
I wear blood-tinted granny glasses against the light.
Sometimes I roar in the night
and hammer my neighbour's wall.

Every day she passes twice,
my eyes bore holes in hers,
that good girl on a man's bike.

If she were here
I would cradle her like a doll.
My eyes boring holes in hers
I would show her my sharp knife.

STARK NAKED BLUES

When I wake up
I can't remember who I hurt.
Memory leaves like a paid lover,
an ache clings.
First trains are loudest,
motorways thick with wiseguys
shitting like bluebottles
on dawn's breast.
It's Winter,
Friday the 13th.
No cornflakes in the bowl
and every reason to be blue.
The postman bangs on the door
with a fistful of holiday brochures
and a final notice from the ESB.
He tells me it's really Friday the 14th,
but what the hell.

These nights of May,
these blue heralds of summer,
revive a familiar ache.
There's no capsule in the cupboard
strong enough, no affinity
between this pain and diagnosis.
I sit by the raised window
watching Venus burn the hills,
the smoky city stretching to the sea,
and wish I was elsewhere.
With eyes squeezed shut
as fierce as gritted teeth
I feel a cut upon my flesh
from a dead past
which should be long healed.
Instead it throbs, and dries
my mouth with a thirst
no liquid on this earth could satisfy.

WHO?

Who came with dirty tricks and lying lips?
Who curved my mother's bones?
Who burned the saplings of the open mind?
Who sealed the wax with telephones?

Let the city hum again,
let the mills grind,
fill the river with whistles
and the voices of honest labour.
I want the nightlights of my childhood back;
my squinted eye throwing creamy spears
at the fake brass holders,
up the rosy wall of the secure room.
I want the kitchen alive with heels and song,
the cold pleasure of silver in the palm,
the street enclosed in its own light,
the children gathered on the kerb
around the painted poles
scaring each other to whiteness,
chasing kisses through 24 pygmy gardens,
two dozen different battlefields,
with the sky minding its own business
and the smell of cooking passing in waves
over the intent heads of the little dreamers.
I want to be returned to the land
of tall legs beneath the table,
one more night in the folds of the laughter
that pealed from the sheds in the wild gardens
under the moonlight that stopped the world.

Who came with keys and private schemes?
Who skied down my father's face?
Who put the blinkers on the wise brown eyes?
Who desecrated this holy place?

FAILED DREAMS

Failed dreams
don't know what to do.
In summer they hang out
on concrete stoops
jeering at traffic
dealing in small talk
and elephantine silences.

Failed dreams
are hopeless in bed.
Their appetite for love
turns to a sour
pounding of bones
a four-eyed struggle
ending in solitude.

Failed dreams
can't keep a friend.
Suspicion flares
at the drop of a hat
and dirt comes cheap.
The shouting on the stairs
breaks bulbs and hearts.

Failed dreams
do not die.
The chicken-hearted losers
desert the sinking flesh
and drag their heels
around the sleeping earth
leaving prints for feet not yet born.

JAYWALKING

It is far too bright.
Weakened by recent events
the sun must have fallen.

Everything in this room
glistens like spit,
the occupants transparent.

Silence, stubborn as a squeezebox
pulled to its limit,
threatens to tear;

the hurried phrase returns
to its original loneliness.

You'll have to go.
I am what I am, she said,
because of your insidious air.

I used to be a nice kid,
strictly legit.
Look at me now,
jaywalking on this busy road.

HOME AND DRY

Pumped with Prozac
I was floating.
Shot down here
I know the menu by heart,
I'm back where I started
shaking hands with the dead.
How could I have forgotten
the terrible silences,
the floored heads,
the ancient wounds,
the busted gramophone,
the twisted nails,
the wheezing trapped
in the thin walls.
Leave the blue pills on the locker,
fill the glass with silt,
time is no healer,
the scum on the river
is thicker, more congealed,
and in the picture house
the same dumb reels
wind round the old projector wheels.

THE BIG PICTURE

One flake of rust
more radiant than sunlight
on the stained-glass of Chartres

One mote of dust
hovering above the peak
of human knowledge

One mutant lark
warbling a wonderful
composition of decay

That's all there is to the picture
we're too frightened to unveil

THE FACE

The face is coming.
It will be perfectly blank,
ordinary, all-tolerant,
capable of being
whatever face your heart desires.
It will be above suspicion.
Its expressions will automatically
translate into your native tongue.
No border will refuse
its bland bewitching eyes
raised on billboards everywhere
as we pass in our adoring millions
with lighter lives and cleaner products,
instilled with the revolutionary fervour
            of face value.

A FOREIGN CHRISTMAS

After the dish of the day,
beans and mash and chicken wings,
I take out the sherry and pour
a tall glass for my sick mother.

On the basement steps, in the concrete yard,
the snow is thick and frozen hard
but the doors, front and back,
are well bolted; the draughts stuffed
with old coats and curtains.

I light the tinsel-curled candle,
plug in the mono portable
and play my mother's favourite songs
from Ireland across the sea.

Over the sweep of the fiddles I hear
the chops and licks of reggae from next door,
and overhead, the thumping of tablas,
the twanging of a lone sitar.

VOODOO DOLL

1 .

At the bottom left-hand corner
of an otherwise empty canvas
there lurks a minuscule panther.
She calls this her *Creature Period*.

2 .

My black buck-toothed skeleton
goes with me everywhere.
Her grip on my ankle
is an anchor.
She plays silly games like
kiss, dare, truth, torture.

3 .

Her ideal city is vermillion
or scarlet, full of smoking manholes.
She knows what hell is like
and where I got my sly brown eyes.

4 .

Her silence is abhorrent
but her screams are worse.
Her whine is all heart,
even her despair is muscular.

5.

She's the queen of the sewer,
Satan's bit on the side.
Her sheets are patterned
with satin plums.
She's easy to find in the dark,
just follow the hissing.

INTANGIBLES INC.

It was cool then,
with wild connotations.
We played with laid-back days
and streets turning no place special
as clocks and watches dribbled numbers.

I stayed in bed for half a month
sniffing laughing gas and ether,
stroking my slender guitarist hands.
You wandered in some Bardo twilight
watching aircraft from the roof.
We were breath and sleep,
Intangibles Inc. The spooky militia.

Two decades have passed;
it is even dreamier now.
Today is the third week
of a lonesome ache,
your moods like celluloid
flipping off and on,
my credentials burned.

The game is turning drastic.
I call you by your name,
you call me by my name.
Our voices encircle each other
like hoops of water.

BYSTANDER

His clothes didn't fit.
Baggy and creaseless
with a whistle in his mouth
he stood in the rain
down on Dog Street
teasing a bird in a cage
enjoying the nervous flutters
of its wings against the bars.
With his right arm in a sling
the butcher looked out at rain
from his closed shop window.
Smelling of cabbage and earth
several female Caesars
with pip eyes and steel hair
gathered round parked cars
gossiping. It was early morning.
The world was descending stairs
lighting stoves
pursuing itself.
After the loud flash the billboards
in the station toppled.
He lost half his face. The scream
of the ambulance closed his remaining eye.

SHRAPNEL

His feet were once the wands
that woke the party
now Dancer is worse than dead.
Puffing on contraband tobacco
he sits by the window of Enzo's Café
stirring a cheap espresso
the shades on his eyes
draining the veg stalls of colour.
The clock on the wall is stopped
at the year in his head
19.54
the year he pulled a knife on his mother
who saw Jesus everywhere.
His skin is dirty yellow
ebbing to bone
weakened by too many failed cures
shrapnel from the great war of dreams.

EDUCATION FOR LIFE

On my last day inside
I had a class of two.
One white boy with a Rasta t-shirt
and a lank kid with serious acne.
Whenever I opened my mouth
they stopped listening
so I listened instead
to their boastings of petty crime.
Then the tall one plucked
a fat cockroach off the wall
laid it on its back on the prison floor
and burned its legs off with a BIC.
Look at the sucker breakdance, he said,
the cockroach spinning, spinning.

DREAM OUTLAW

as he drifts towards sleep I begin to awaken

now I'm up
pacing the threadbare carpet
of this temporary room

above me a jet soars away
to some temperate region
while across the street
a gigantic cigarette with glowing neon tip
puffs its electrical way down to the filter
relighting and blooming this hideout
with a fake pink smoke without fire

he doesn't know it
but I've strangled a child
stuffed its little body in a boiler

he doesn't know it
but I hit it harder than I meant
the crack of its skull
like accidently stomping on a snail

he doesn't know it
but when he wakes up
it is my guilt that will make him suffer

LOST CHILDREN

I was walking too fast
when I lost them.
My mind, a crowded Christmas city,
streamed with tinsel and hype.
The words I should have said
lodged in my throat,
cascaded in my gut.
Too busy with abstract options
I was wrapped up in the relevance
of the brush I bought that painted me
a dirty shade of grey. I wasn't thinking,
didn't notice the importance of the time.
The warm urgency of their hands in mine
passed cleanly through my flesh,
and when I looked around they were gone.
Ten years were gone and I was walking alone
down an avenue of London planes
in a Dublin I reached by default.
Each night I dream of them falling into holes,
floating through space, hiding in leafy trees,
running through one door as I come through another.

EVEN LOVE IN A CAGE

Even love in a cage can be sweet.
But sooner or later
the shadows of the bars
won't wash from the skin.

You begin to whine,
and when your face grows
longer than a sleepless night
your loving keeper,
overcome by mercy,
slips the lock.

You're free. You test the dust
with a tentative paw
and it feels good, so you stalk
to the ring's circumference,
and smelling fresh game in the cool dusk
you go back to the world of the hunt.

The circus of the seasons rolls.
You grow sick of the immense rivers,
the taste of blood, the unconfining skies,
the pulpy stench of the forests,
the impermanent shelters.

Older, leaner, you follow and follow
the unforgettable scent of your keeper's hand
searching for the steel door
that swings inward to that sweet, narrow bed,
and you say, tilt to me your real red lip,
let me live in its unruffled shadow.

A BIG HAND

swaddled in dustdrifts under the bed
my suitcase packed for seven years
ready to go when the whistle blows
waiting at the door for a big hand

not the sealed decks
that the same night rains

not the candy angels
that melt at sunrise

not the glow of another glass
that leads to torment

not the immense ideas
aborted by sleep and torpor

not the pig love
that guzzles the gentle finger

not the cheap line
that costs too dear

not the unbearable silence
of some morning after

not the easy rigmarole
of permanent guile

but a big hand with its generous aces
all beautiful four without a joker

FUEL

She gave me slim blue pages
and a jar of pens.

Write it down, she said,
memory is an eagle in full flight
and the past is a lamb.
The tongue of memory
anticipates the gravy,
the beak of memory slobbers,
the wings of memory spread wide.
Taste it, she said,
your own cooked goose.
Wrap the tough skin, the tender breast,
the bones, the giblets and the miles of fat,
wrap them slowly in the slim blue pages,
fuel your hunger.

HONEYCOMB HOUSE

On that winter's morning
utterly defeated, my heart
a big bass drum inside my shirt,
the deadly sound in the Green
of an old man palpitating,
a pint-size shadow on a bench,
I saw a young boy pass by
and caught the loaded stare
of his betrayed innocence.
What I had lost
would stay lost forever,
the rotten rooms of the past
become the floss of the future,
so I counted what I had rescued
from the great destructive London fire,
the sour lip, the shocked
eye of the terminal hurt,
and I prayed for a carnal saviour
to descend and unscrew my pain.
Then, before going down for the 3rd time,
the honeycomb house appeared before me,
and the glare of the sun on its glass
said, *strike, strike against the waves,*
and every gasp I gasped became a muscle,
even my toenails clawed the rising tide,
not yet, not yet, imagination cried.
So I climbed the stairs and turned the key,
and my children, Dust and Silence,
ran to me; *daddy's home, daddy's home.*

QUARTET

The Love

From new moon to new moon
your love is a bride
waiting in a barren land.
By the wayside you sit
calling birds of prey from the east
and binding them onto your gown,
painfully, as a faithful bride would.

The Beauty

Your nest is set amongst the stars
but here on earth your throne
is cold stone, fire.
To be near you
I will put hooks in my jaws,
cut wings in my wrists.

The Dream

Years come and years go
but the dream is one.
It was sprouted long ago from one stalk.
The moon and eleven stars
bowed over the earth,
and high, beyond measure, the dream was.

The Passing

We separated the lambs and laid the rods.
We dwelt here, stopped and filled our hands with pain.
Now, these pillars between us witness our dissolution,
drive us like smoke before wind, forget we ever
   touched.

MAYFLY

don't need no mouth
no belly
for my one-day dance

around this green and fecund lake
that's loud with shivering pap
and smells of being born

as I look down from hungry eyes
the hours are pressing
but the sight's a miracle

so I sow my genes and flutter
on this trampoline of water

drawing the sky and the sour lilies
into the frame of a brief life
flying on slowing wings to sundown